MALE . . .

Why is a woman's blind date like a snow-storm?

(see p. 9)

What did the flasher say to the woman in February?

(see p. 28)

Why's a tight pair of pants like a cheap hotel?

(see p. 37)

. . . FEMALE . . .

What do you call two women in the freezer?

(see p. 74)

What's harder than getting six pregnant women in a Volkswagen?

(see p. 83)

What should a woman give the man who has everything?

(see p. 100)

. . . A

W9-CJT-904

Also by Blanche Knott
Published by St. Martin's Paperbacks

Blanche Knott's
Book of Truly Tasteless Anatomy Jokes
Vol. II

SMP

ST. MARTIN'S PAPERBACKS

BLANCHE KNOTT'S TRULY TASTELESS ANATOMY JOKES, VOLUME II

ISBN: 0-312-92421-6

Printed in the United States of America

St. Martin's Paperbacks edition/February 1991

10 9 8 7 6 5 4 3 2 1

For Andrew, partner in crime

PART ONE:
MALE ANATOMY

Did you hear about the young boy whose mother caught him jerking off in the bathroom? She told him to stop because he'd go blind, and he asked if he could keep going till he needed glasses.

•

One night after work, Scott is greeted at the door by his wife clad in a flimsy negligee. Before he has a chance to remove his coat, she falls to her knees, yanks his fly down, pulls his dick out and proceeds to give him a wonderful, sloppy blowjob.

"All right!" Scott sighs. "What happened to the car?"

•

George got a terrible sunburn on the nude beach, and later that day found lovemaking with his girlfriend excruciatingly painful. Going into the kitchen, he poured himself a tall glass of cold milk and inserted his sore penis.

"Aha," said the girl, watching from the doorway. "I've always wanted to know how you reloaded that thing!"

•

A new lumberjack had just finished his first month of work in the godforsaken wilds of Alaska, where no women were to be found for hundreds of miles. Finally he couldn't take it anymore, so he overcame his embarrassment and asked the foreman what the other fellows did to relieve the pressure.

"Try the hole in the barrel outside the shower," suggested the foreman. "The other guys swear by it."

Dubious but figuring he had nothing to lose, the lumberjack took the advice. To his astonishment, it was the best sexual experience of his life. "That barrel is fantastic!" he reported glowingly. "I'm not gonna miss a day from now on."

"Except Wednesday," corrected the foreman.

"Why not Wednesday?" asked the puzzled lumberjack.

"That's your day in the barrel."

•

A man taking a tour through hell with the devil saw a room filled with wine bottles and beautiful, naked women.

"I could have a good time in that room," he snickered.

"That's what you think," said the devil, winking slyly. "See those wine bottles? They all have holes in the bottom."

He pointed again. "See those women? They don't!"

•

Very horny but also very broke, Sam managed to scrape up two bucks and walk down to the local whorehouse. Looking at his meager offering, the madam burst out laughing. But being a good-natured sort, she informed him that there was in fact a special room for customers on a tight budget. Sam nodded gratefully, and was shown into a small, grimy room containing only a full-length mirror and a duck. No way am I going to fuck a duck, he thought to himself. But after a while his horny state got the better of him, and, figuring he'd try anything once, he went for the duck.

A week later Sam was even hornier, but this time he had only a dollar to his name.

"Sorry, buddy, but you can't get laid for a lousy dollar," the madam informed him. "But you can see a good show."

Sam handed over his money and was led to a room in which several men were looking through a one-way window and roaring at the spectacle of a man getting it on with a nanny goat. Recalling last week's experience and feeling vaguely uncomfortable, Sam said defensively, "I don't see what's so funny, fellas."

One of the spectators turned to him. "You've got a point, pal," he admitted. "Last week we had a guy doing it with a duck, and *that* was a riot!"

•

A young boy, head hung in submission, sat across from a priest in the church confessional. "Forgive me, Father, for I have sinned," he lamented. "I've been having sex with some of the animals on our farm."

"Hmm," muttered the priest. "Were these animals male or female?"

"What the hell do you think I am," screamed the boy, "a faggot?"

•

What are the five worst things about being a penis?

1) You have a hole in your head.

2) You have permanent ring-around-the-collar.

3) Your next-door neighbors are two nuts and an asshole.

4) Your best friend is a cunt.

5) And every time you get excited, you throw up.

•

A man out for his daily constitutional runs into a young girl crying her eyes out. "What's wrong?" he asks sympathetically.

"Leroy's dead!" she wails.

A few more blocks down the street, he comes across a group of women, all in tears. "Leroy's dead!" they're shrieking. "Leroy's gone."

Continuing on his walk, he decides to stop in at the local funeral parlor to ask the undertaker what all the fuss is about. Without saying a word, the undertaker pulls a sheet off the table next to him and exposes a naked male body, unremarkable except for its fourteen-inch penis.

"Is that Leroy?"

The undertaker nods.

"Hey, I'll give you fifty dollars for that guy's dick."

The undertaker nods.

Stuffing the dick in a paper bag, the fellow runs home to his wife, bounds up the stairs and shouts, "You're not going to believe what I've got in this bag."

The curious wife takes the bag from her husband, peeks inside and falls to her knees with a heartrending scream. "Leroy's dead!"

•

Why is life like a penis?

Because when it's soft it's hard to beat, but when it's hard you get screwed.

•

"Hey, pal," the irate druggist shouted, "put that cigar out while you're in my store!"

"I bought this cigar here," complained the customer.

"Big deal," rejoined the druggist. "We sell condoms too."

•

Being a virgin, Bob was very nervous about his upcoming wedding night, so he decided to seek the advice of his friend John, who was quite the local Romeo. "Just relax, Bob," counseled John. "After all, you grew up on a farm— just do like the dogs do."

Right after the honeymoon the bride stormed over to her mother's house in tears and announced that she wasn't going to live under the same roof as Bob for even one more night. "He's totally disgusting!" she wailed.

At first Bob's bride resisted her mother's attempts to find out the exact nature of the problem, but finally she broke down. "Ma, he doesn't know anything at all about how to be romantic, how to make love . . . He just keeps smelling my ass and pissing on the bedpost!"

•

Why is a woman's blind date like a snowstorm?

She never knows how many inches she'll get, or how long it will last.

•

What's 68?

That's when she goes down on you and you owe her one.

•

Define wet dream.

Coming unscrewed.

•

An ambitious hostess decided to throw a costume party at which each guest had to dress up as an emotion. She was at the door to greet the first guest, who was dressed head to toe in blue.

"I get it," she cried happily. "You've got the blues, right?" The guest nodded, and she turned to the couple behind him, which was dressed completely in green.

"Green with envy?" she guessed. The couple nodded and went inside.

The next guest showed up completely naked except for a bowl of custard which had been strapped over his penis. "And what could you be?" asked the puzzled hostess.

He replied with a grin, "I'm fucking disgusted!"

•

"Dad," whispered the young man on the eve of his wedding, "what am I supposed to do? I'm a little nervous."

"Don't worry about a thing," consoled the understanding father. "All you have to do is take that thing you used to play with when you were a little boy and stick it where your wife urinates."

"Wow, that sounds easy enough. Thanks, Dad," the fellow said confidently. He hung up the phone and threw his G.I. Joe doll in the toilet.

•

What's this? (Open your mouth wide and stick out your tongue.)

Blowjobber's cramp.

•

While in the midst of a passionate embrace with a prostitute, the admiral asked, "Well, how'm I doing, mate?"

"Oh, I'd say you're doing about three knots," the hooker answered.

"Eh matey, what do you mean by three knots?" he queried with a leer.

"You're not hard, you're not in, and you're not getting a refund."

•

A guest at nudist camp received a letter from his mother in which she asked for his photograph. Since the only pictures he had at the time had been taken in the nude, he cut one in half and mailed her the top half.

His mom wrote back to thank him for the photo and asked whether he could send one to his grandmother as well. Since Grandma's practically blind, why ruin another photo? reasoned the young man to himself. And he mailed off the bottom half.

"Thanks for the picture," wrote Grandma, "but your haircut makes your nose look long."

•

"Stop!" screamed Nancy as her boyfriend fucked her up the ass. "It hurts!"

"You're crazy," Rambo replied. "It feels great!"

11

A woman went into the neighborhood grocery store and asked the proprietor for a can of cat food. Knowing that she didn't own a cat, the grocer couldn't resist inquiring about the purchase.

"Oh, it's for my husband," she explained.

The grocer was shocked. "You can't feed cat food to your husband. It might kill him!"

"I've been giving it to him for a week now and it obviously agrees with him," she replied evenly, and changed the subject to the weather.

Every week or so she came in and stocked up on cat food. And one day the grocer happened to be scanning the obituary column of the local paper and noticed that her husband had passed away. When the woman next came into the store, he offered his condolences.

"I was awfully sorry to read about your husband—but I told you if you kept giving him cat food it'd kill him."

"Oh, it wasn't the cat food that killed him," the new widow informed the grocer matter-of-factly. "He broke his neck trying to lick his ass."

•

The unemployed porno star was looking for someone to represent him. "Do you have an eight-by-ten?" asked an agent.

"Shit," said the actor, "if I had an eight-by-ten, I wouldn't be out of work."

Then there was the woman who was suing for divorce on the grounds of "hobosexuality."

"Don't you mean 'homosexuality'?" inquired her friend delicately.

"Nope," snapped the malcontent wife. "He's a bum fuck."

•

When sixteen-year-old Ernie came home with the news that he'd gotten laid for the first time, his mother was less than pleased. Slapping him across the face, she sent him off to his room without any supper.

When Ernie's father got home and heard the news, he went up to see his son.

"Well, my boy," he admonished, secretly pleased, "I hope you learned something from this experience."

"You bet I did," admitted his son. "Next time I use Vaseline—my ass is killing me!"

•

The traveling salesman checked into a futuristic motel. Realizing he needed a trim before the next day's big meeting, he called down to the desk clerk to ask if there was a barber on the premises. "I'm afraid not, sir," the clerk told him apologetically, "but down the hall is a vending machine that should serve your purposes."

Skeptical but intrigued, the salesman located the appropriate machine, inserted fifty cents, and stuck his head in the opening, at which the machine started to buzz and whir. Fifteen seconds later the salesman pulled out his head and surveyed his reflection, which reflected the best haircut of his life.

Two feet away was another machine with a sign that read, "Manicures—25 cents." Why not? thought the salesman. He paid the money, inserted his hands into the slot, and pulled them out perfectly manicured.

The next machine had a huge sign that read, "This Machine Provides What Men Need Most When Away from Their Wives—50 cents." The salesman looked both ways, put in fifty cents, unzipped his fly, and stuck his dick into the opening. When the machine started buzzing, the guy let out a shriek of agony. Fifteen seconds later it shut off and, with trembling hands, the salesman was able to withdraw his penis . . . now with a button sewed to the tip.

•

Walking along a deserted beach, a man finds an empty bottle which he picks up and rubs. Sure enough a genie appears and offers the man two wishes.

"I wish I were always hard and could get all the ass I wanted," he informs the genie.

"Whatever turns you on," the genie replies, and turns the man into a toilet seat.

•

A guy went into the corner drugstore and boasted that two lovely young stewardesses were coming to spend the whole weekend at his apartment. "I need something to get it hard and keep it hard—for the whole two days," he confided to the pharmacist.

The druggist insisted that he couldn't dispense any such drug without a prescription, but after a long and detailed inventory of the stewardesses' charms, he relented and sold the guy a small bottle of lotion. "Use it sparingly," he cautioned.

When he opened the drugstore on Monday morning, the pharmacist was horrified to see the guy crawling across the sidewalk toward him, exhausted and bleeding, his clothes in tatters.

As he reached the door, the battered customer croaked, "Please, Doc, you gotta give me some Ben-Gay."

"Christ, man," exclaimed the pharmacist, "you can't put Ben-Gay on your pecker. It'll hurt like hell!"

"It's not for my pecker," the fellow groaned, "it's for my elbow. The girls never showed up."

•

An hour after checking into the motel, the traveling salesman stormed up to the front desk. "What kind of chickenshit joint are you running?" he demanded.

"What's the problem, sir?" stammered the confused desk clerk.

"I went up to my room, unlocked the door, and there was a man holding a gun," blustered the irate guest. "He told me to get on my knees and give him a blowjob or he'd blast my brains all over the room."

"Oh, my God," gasped the clerk, shocked and embarrassed. "What did you do?"

The salesman screamed, "Well, you didn't hear any shots, did you?"

•

A certain college professor was notorious for getting off the lecture topic and on to his favorite subject: the evils of marijuana. Off he went one day into the inventory of horrors. "Used regularly, pot can cause psychic disorientation, sterility, cancer, castration—"

"Now just a minute, Prof," interrupted a long-haired student. *"Castration?"*

"You bet, son," replied the teacher smugly. "Just suppose your girlfriend gets the munchies . . ."

•

What's the coldest part of an Eskimo?

His balls—because they're two below.

•

Two winos, Ricky and Billy, woke up in an alley in dire need of a drink but with only sixty cents between them.

"Say, I got an idea," proposed Ricky. He proceeded to invest their capital in a hot dog from a corner vendor, then pulled Billy into the nearest bar and ordered a round of drinks. Downing them and observing the waitress heading over with the bill, Ricky deftly pulled out the hot dog, inserted the end in Billy's fly, and proceeded to suck on it vigorously.

"Get the hell outta here, you goddamn queers!" yelled the bartender.

This worked equally well at the next bar, and the next, and the next—in fact, all through the day—and when they made it back to the alley, they were dead drunk. "Shee what ya can do with a hot dog?" Ricky crowed cheerfully.

"What hot dog?" giggled Billy. "We losht da hot dog after da third bar."

•

What did the stewardess say to the flasher?

"I asked for your ticket, not your stub."

•

Why do boys run faster than girls?

They have two ball bearings and a stick shift.

·

Jim was having an affair with his boss's wife, and one afternoon they were going at it when they heard footsteps on the stairs.

"Quick," hissed his lover, "jump out the window."

Fortunately, it was a first-floor apartment, and even more fortunately, the New York City Marathon happened to be passing by, so Jim just fell into step with the pack.

"Tell me something," gasped the man running next to him, "do you always wear a condom when you run?"

Thinking fast, Jim replied, "Only when it looks like rain."

·

A traveler stopped in a little backwoods restaurant for lunch, after which he inquired the way to the rest room. Going around to the back of the building, he found the outhouse and took a shit, only to discover that no toilet paper had been provided. But a sign on the wall read, WIPE YOURSELF WITH YOUR FINGER AND INSERT IT IN THIS HOLE. IT WILL BE CLEANED WITH GREAT ATTENTION. So he followed the instructions, and stuck his finger through the hole.

On the other side of the wall, a little boy holding two bricks clapped them together.

Howling with pain and surprise, the man yanked back his hand and popped the injured finger into his mouth.

•

When is it justified for a woman to spit in a man's face?

When his mustache is on fire.

•

Why can't Gypsies have children?

Because the men have crystal balls.

•

The customer came up to the pharmacist indignantly. "Last Friday I ordered twelve dozen rubbers," he said angrily, "and when I got home I found I'd been shorted a dozen."

"Gee," returned the pharmacist drily, "I hope I didn't ruin your weekend."

•

This fellow had been assured by his fiancée that she was a virgin, but given the state of modern morals, he didn't completely trust her. So he devised a little quiz for their wedding night. Pulling down his pajamas, he asked, "Honey, can you tell me what this is?"

"A wee-wee," she answered coyly.

Delighted by her naiveté, the new husband corrected her gently. "No, sweetheart. It's a penis."

"Uh-uh, it's a wee-wee," insisted his bride, shaking her head.

Slightly annoyed, he shook his head. "It's time for you to learn a few things, dearest. Now, this is a penis."

"No way," she retorted. "It's not half as big as some of the penises I've seen."

•

What's the big risk behind electric blankets?
    Wet dreams.

•

As a last resort, Mr. Jones went to the sex therapist, confiding that his and his wife's sex life was abysmal.

Leaning back in his big leather chair and nodding gravely, the doctor advised, "Have a few martinis first, to loosen things up a bit. Then let your mind roam over the possibilities; think about how exciting you used to find the whole business."

The doctor's gaze strayed out the office window into the courtyard, where two dogs happened to be screwing vigorously. "You see—just look at the vitality and vigor of those animals," the doctor exhorted. "Go home and reflect on their spontaneity over a few drinks. I'll see you in two weeks."

Two weeks later the therapist asked, "Well? How'd it go?"

"Terribly," answered the patient glumly. "It took seven martinis just to get her out in the yard."

•

When Mike came into the doctor's office for his test results, the doctor told him he had some good news and some bad news.

"I'll take the good news first," requested the patient.

"Your penis is going to grow two inches in length and an inch in circumference."

"That's terrific," Mike exclaimed, breaking into a big smile. "So what could be bad?"

The doctor answered, "Malignant."

•

What has 196 teeth and holds back a monster?
  My zipper.

•

What's the definition of a loser?
  Someone a hooker tells, "Not now—I have a headache."

•

The American tourist walked into a restaurant in Madrid and sat down to look the menu over. It was all in Spanish, so he decided to see what people around him were eating that looked good. And right next to him was a man eating these two *huge* bull's balls. Feeling adventurous, he told the waiter, "I'd like to have the same as that fellow, please."

"I'm sorry, señor," the waiter informed him apologetically, "but those must be ordered a day in advance."

So the tourist placed his order, and came in the next day ready for a feast. When the waiter served him a plate on which sat two tiny balls, he spluttered, "What the hell's this? It's not what I saw that man eating at the table next to me last night!"

The waiter shrugged. "Sometimes, señor, the *bull* wins."

•

Two men were standing at adjacent urinals when one said to the other, "I'll bet you were born in Newark, Ohio."

"Why, that's right," said the second man in surprise.

"And I'll bet you were circumcised when you were three days old."

"Right again. But how'd you—"

"And I'll bet it was done by old Doc Steadman."

"Well, yes, but how did you know?" asked the second man in amazement.

"Well, old Doc always cut them at a sixty-degree angle," explained the first guy, "and you're pissing on my shoe."

•

How did Captain Hook die?
  Jock itch.

•

What do you call sperm from a reporter?
  Journaljism.

•

What did the doctor say to the nervous patient about his upcoming circumcision?
  "It won't be long now."

•

Hungry for company, the young couple is delighted when a spaceship lands on their very isolated farm. Out steps a young, very humanoid, Martian couple. They get to talking and soon the wife invites the Martians to dinner. And over dinner the conversation is so stimulating and all four get along so well that they decide to swap partners for the night.

The farmer's wife and the male Martian get the master bedroom, and when he undresses she sees that his phallus is very small indeed. "What are you going to do with that?" she can't resist asking.

"Watch," he says smartly. He twists his right ear and his penis suddenly grows to eighteen inches in length—but it's still as skinny as a pencil. And again the farmer's wife can't suppress a disparaging comment.

So the Martian twists his left ear, at which his prick grows thick as a sausage. And he and the woman proceed to screw like crazy all night long.

After cordial farewells and promises to write, the next morning the Martian couple takes off. Immediately the farmer turns to his wife. "Well, honey? So how was it?"

"It was fabulous, really out of this world," reports the wife with a big smile. "How about you?"

"Nothing special," admits the farmer. "Kinda weird in fact. All night long she kept playing with my ears."

•

A well-dressed man walked into a nice bar. Ordering two martinis, he drank one down and proceeded to pour the second on his hand. Unable to contain his curiosity, the bartender leaned over. "I hope you don't mind me asking, sir, but why'd you just waste a perfectly good drink?"

The man explained, "I just want to get my date drunk."

●

A man once explained to me that his penis was four inches. "Now some women like it," he went on, "but others complain it's just too wide."

●

During his monthly visit to the corner barbershop, this fellow asked his barber for any suggestions on how to treat his increasing baldness. After a brief pause, the barber leaned over and confided that the best thing he'd come across was, er, female juices.

"But you're balder than I am," protested the customer.

"True," admitted the barber, "but you've gotta admit I've got one hell of a mustache!"

●

Whom should you see if your hand isn't enough?

A wet nurse.

●

The Steinbergs decided to hold a bris for their son, but were shocked when the rabbi quoted them a fee of $135. "Too much," they said, and went to a moyel, who wanted $125. "Too much," they said, and decided to do it themselves, getting out a big knife.

Two minutes later, they said, "Too much."

•

If a man's case of VD is called herpes, what's it called when his wife catches it?

Hispies.

•

When the extremely obese man showed up for his doctor's appointment, he claimed he'd tried every possible way to lose weight. So the doctor proposed a radical diet: anal feeding. Reassuring his patient that he wouldn't starve to death, the doctor explained that adequate nutrients would be absorbed through the rectal walls, and that weight loss was virtually guaranteed.

A month later the patient came in for his follow-up appointment; sure enough, he was down from 360 to a trim 175 pounds. Showing him into his office and observing that the one-time fatty was bouncing up and down in his seat energetically, the doctor asked how he was feeling.

"Just fine, Doc, never better," was the patient's cheerful reply.

"Well then, would you mind explaining why

you're bouncing up and down like that?" asked the puzzled doctor.

"Just chewing some gum!"

•

A man was experiencing chronic infections, so he took his urologist's advice and entered the hospital for a routine circumcision. When he came to, he was perturbed to see a large group of doctors standing around his hospital bed. "What's up, Doc?" he asked nervously.

"Uh, well . . . there's been a bit of a mix-up," admitted his surgeon. "I'm afraid that instead of a circumcision, we performed a sex-change operation on you. You now have a very nice vagina instead of a penis."

"What!" gasped the patient. "You mean I'll never experience another erection?"

"Oh, I'm sure you *will*," reassured the doctor, "only it'll be somebody else's."

•

Three men stopped at a big house in the country to ask for lodging for the night. The owner of the house was very obliging, but as she showed them to their rooms, she had one request: that they not look inside the big closet on the landing.

All night long her guests resisted temptation, but the next morning they opened the closet doors and found themselves looking at a collection of hundreds of penises nailed to the shelves and sides. "Well, fellas, you asked for it," said their hostess, coming up behind them. Turning to the man closest to her, she asked, "What does your father do?"

"My dad's a butcher," he stammered.

The woman took a meat cleaver, chopped off his dick, and nailed it to the wall. "And what does your father do?" she asked, turning to her second guest.

"He's a carpenter," he quavered.

So the woman took a jigsaw, sawed off his cock, and nailed it to the wall. "And yours?" she asked the third man.

"My dad's a lollipop manufacturer," he replied with a grin. "You're going to have to suck mine off."

•

Heard about the new generic rubbers?

They're for cheap fuckers.

•

What did the flasher say to the woman in sub-zero weather?

"It's so cold—should I just describe myself?"

•

An eight-year-old boy was charged with the rape of a twenty-nine-year-old woman, and though the charge seemed highly unlikely, the state's evidence was overwhelming. As a last, desperate move, the defense counsel came over to his client on the witness stand, pulled down his pants, and grabbed the little boy's tiny penis. "Ladies and gentlemen," the lawyer cried, gesturing toward the jury box, "surely you cannot believe that such a small, as yet undeveloped organ is sexually mature?" Growing more agitated, he went on, "How could it be capable even of erection, let alone the rape of a full grown—"

"WATCH IT!" yelped the kid from the stand. "One more shake and you'll lose the case."

•

Once upon a time King Arthur was preparing for a long campaign. Wanting to make sure the lovely Guinevere was safe from temptation, the king had her fitted with an ingenious chastity belt designed to amputate anything attempting penetration, and off he rode to battle with a clear heart.

Returning victorious six months later, the suspicious ruler ordered all the palace retainers to drop their pants in the courtyard. One by one, Arthur saw stumps where their penises had been, except for one man who stood intact at the end of the line. "At least one amongst you is virtuous enough to resist temptation: a man of honor," cried the king joyfully, throwing his arms around his loyal retainer. "And what is your name?"

The man blushed and replied, "Aaaghkghulh."

•

Edith and Roberta were hanging out their laundry in their backyards when the talk came around to why their neighbor's laundry never got rained on. So when Marcia came out with her laundry basket, Roberta asked her how come she always seemed to know the forecast. "Your laundry's never hanging out when it starts to rain," she pointed out in an aggrieved tone.

Marcia leaned over the fence and winked at her two friends. "When I wake up in the morning I look over at Buddy," she explained. "If his penis is hanging over his right leg, I know it's going to be fair weather and I come right out with my laundry. On the other hand, if it's hanging left, for sure it's going to rain, so I hang it up inside."

"Well, smarty-pants," said Edith, "what if Buddy's got a hard-on?"

"Honey," replied Marcia with a smile, "on a day like *that* you don't do the *laundry.*"

•

What's the problem with oral sex?
The view.

•

What's six inches long that women love?
  Folding money.

•

One morning a milkman called on one of his regular customers and was surprised to see a white bedsheet with a hole in the middle hanging up in her living room. The housewife explained that she'd had a party the night before. They had played a game called "Who's Who," in which each of the men had put their equipment through the hole and the women had tried to guess their identity.

"Gee, that sounds like fun," said the milkman. "Sure wish I'd been there."

"You should have been," the housewife informed him. "Your name came up three times."

•

An assembly-line worker became increasingly obsessed with a desire to stick his penis into the pickle slicer. Finally, worried that he'd be unable to contain the desire, he sought the advice of a psychiatrist.

"You know, I had a case not unlike this one a few months ago," said Dr. Bernstein, thoughtfully rubbing his beard, "a man who kept wanting to put his hand on a hot stove."

"So what happened?" asked the factory worker.

"He went ahead and did it," confessed the doctor, "and he burned himself, but he never had the desire again. So my advice is to go ahead and follow your impulse in order to free yourself of it."

"Okay, Doc." And the patient left.

At his next appointment the doctor asked what had happened.

"I took your advice," said the man, "and stuck my penis into the pickle slicer."

"And then what?" asked the psychiatrist, leaning forward eagerly.

"We both got fired."

•

Who's the most popular guy in the nudist camp?

The one who can carry two cups of coffee and a dozen doughnuts at the same time.

•

A man walks into his doctor's office and the receptionist gives him a form to fill out and asks him what his problem is. He says, "I've got something wrong with my cock."

"Please watch your language!" scolds the receptionist. "There are women and children in the waiting room."

The would-be patient leaves the office, only to

return a few minutes later and say to the receptionist, "I've got a problem with my ear."

"Now that's much better," says the receptionist. "What's wrong with it?"

"I can't piss out of it."

•

What do you call a mountain climber who's had a vasectomy?

Dry sack on the rocks.

•

How do you say "premature ejaculation" in French?

"Ooh la la—so soon?"

•

What do you call a man with no dick?

A sucker.

•

The newlyweds were undressing in their honeymoon suite on the wedding night. The new husband, who was a big bruiser of a guy, tossed his pants over to his wife and said, "Here, put these on."

Puzzled, she pulled them on and said, "These would fit two of me—I can't wear these pants."

"That's right," said the husband, "and don't

you forget it. I'm the one who wears the pants in this family."

With that the wife threw her panties over to his side of the bed and demanded, "Try these on."

Finding he could only get them up as far as his knees, her husband said, "Hell, I can't even get *into* your panties.

"That's right," she snapped, "and that's the way it's going to be until your goddamn attitude changes."

•

What's the definition of a macho?

Someone who's been circumcised with pinking shears.

•

What makes a man think he's so great?

He has a belly button that won't work.

He has tits that won't give milk.

He has a cock that won't crow.

He has balls that won't roll.

He has an ass that won't carry a thing.

Hey, what are you smiling for? Your pussy won't catch mice.

•

What do you call a two-hundred-foot-long rubber?

A condominium.

Did you hear about the guy with five dicks?
His pants fit like a glove.

•

Why do men swim faster than women?
Because they have a rudder.

•

Little Billy asked his father, "Dad, what's a penis?"

Without missing a beat, his father unzipped his fly, pulled it out, and said, "Son, *this* is a penis. And, I might add, it's a perfect penis."

"Thanks, Dad," said little Billy, and ran over to his best friend's house to tell him about this new revelation.

"Really?" said his friend in amazement. "Well, what did he show you?"

"This," said the little boy, unzipping his own pants and taking out his prick. "And you know what? If it were just a little bit shorter, it'd be just as perfect as my dad's."

•

A woman had a big, old German shepherd that snored so loudly she could never hear her soap operas in the afternoon. Over coffee one morning she happened to mention the problem to her neighbor, who whispered confidentially that she had just the solution. "The next time it happens, tie a ribbon around his balls and he'll stop," said the neighbor. "He won't even wake up."

That afternoon, during the first few minutes of *As the World Turns*, the dog came in and flopped down in front of the TV. Within three minutes he had turned onto his back and begun snoring deeply, so the woman ran to her sewing room and grabbed a red ribbon. Sure enough, the neighbor was right: when the ribbon was tied around his nuts, the dog stopped snoring.

That very night was her husband's bowling night, and he came home very late and very drunk. He fell into bed, rolled onto his back, and began to snore loudly, and as his wife lay there sleepless, her neighbor's suggestion came to mind a second time. Fetching a blue ribbon from her sewing box, she tied it around her husband's balls. He fell silent and never stirred.

Later on that night the husband woke up to take a leak. Still pretty drunk, he staggered down the hall, let the dog out, and went to pee. Looking down at his cock, he noticed the blue ribbon, and when he let the dog back in, he noticed the red one. "Woofer," he said blurrily, "I don't know where we've been . . . but at least we came in first and second."

•

Why did God make man first?

He didn't want a woman looking over his shoulder.

•

Why's a tight pair of pants like a cheap hotel?

There's no ball room.

•

Hey there, have you ever read the print at the end of a condom?

No? Oh, I see . . . you never had to unroll it that far.

•

A recent poll uncovered the fact that 90% of all men masturbate in the shower. The other 10% sing. Do you know what they sing?

You say you don't know? I didn't think so . . .

•

A couple of truck drivers met at a diner on an interstate. "Yo, Jack," said one to the other, "I haven't seen you in months. How're you doing? Getting any on the side?"

Jack sighed wearily and confessed, "I haven't had any in so long I didn't know they'd moved it."

•

A traveling salesman was looking for a place to spend the night, and a local farmer offered to take him in if he didn't mind sharing quarters with his daughter. The salesman said that would be fine.

A few months later the salesman received the following letter from the farmer:

> Are you the guy who did the pushin'?
> Left the grease spots on the cushion?
> Left the footprints on the dashboard upside down?
> Ever since you left my Nellie
> She's been swellin' 'round the belly
> So you'd better come back to this here town.

The salesman replied by return mail:

> Yes I'm the guy who did the pushin'
> Left the grease spots on the cushion
> Left the footprints on the dashboard upside down.
> Ever since I left your Venus
> I've been itching round the penis,
> So I think we're pretty even all around.

●

A young couple was parked on Lovers Lane and the young man turned admiringly to his pretty date and said, "Gee, you smell good. You wearing perfume or something?"

The girl blushed charmingly and confessed

that she was wearing a new scent that she'd bought especially with him in mind. "You smell good too," she told him. "What have you got on?"

"Well, I have a hard-on," blurted the young man, "but I didn't know you could smell it."

•

What's long and red and hard and comes with balls?

A baseball bat.

•

And what did one ball say to the other?

"Why should we hang? It was Peter that did all the shooting."

•

A little girl walked into the bathroom, saw her father in the shower, and ran to her mother screaming, "Mommy, Mommy! Daddy has a big ugly worm hanging out of his wee-wee!"

"That isn't a worm, sweetheart," said her mother reassuringly. "That's part of your daddy's body, and a very important part. If your daddy didn't have one of those, you wouldn't be here."

Pausing thoughtfully, the woman added, "And come to think of it . . . neither would I."

•

Marvin liked to hang out at the beach, and he couldn't help noticing this other guy who had girls all around him like bees around a flower. Finally Marvin went over to shoot the bull with the lifeguard. "Some guys have all the luck, eh?" he commented. "Just look at that one; you know he's getting more pussy than any man can handle. How come I'm not making out like him?"

"You really want to know?" said the lifeguard with a grin. "The next time you come down to the beach, try putting a potato in your bathing suit."

This sounded like a good suggestion to Marvin, so he couldn't understand why everyone was cracking up when he took his next stroll in the surf. "Hey, man, all I did was follow your advice," he complained to the lifeguard. "How come everyone's laughing at me?"

The lifeguard leaned forward and whispered, "The potato's supposed to go in the *front* of your suit."

•

Having been at sea for three months, the sailor was extremely horny when his ship reached port. Heading straight to the nearest whorehouse, he asked the price.

"Seventy-five bucks," replied the madam.

It seemed pretty steep, but he was desperate. Paying up, he was shown to an empty room.

When the whore opened the door, she saw the sailor masturbating furiously on the bed. "Stop, stop," she cried. "What the hell're you doing?"

"Think about it, honey," replied the sailor. "For seventy-five bucks you don't think I'm going to let you have the easy one, do you?"

•

Joe was in the corner bar having a few when his friend Phil dropped in and joined him. It didn't take long for Phil to notice a string hanging out of the back of Joe's shirt collar that his friend kept tugging on.

Finally Phil couldn't contain his curiousity, and asked, "What the hell's that string for?"

"Two weeks ago I had a date with that dish, Linda," Joe explained, "and when I got her into the sack, would you believe I couldn't perform? Made me so mad that I tied this string to my dick, and every time I think of how it let me down, I pull the string and make it kiss my ass."

•

After the wedding young Ramona was taken upstairs by her groom, but in less than five minutes she came running downstairs to the kitchen where her mother was making lasagna. "Mama, Mama," the young virgin wailed, "he's got hair all over his chest!"

"He's-a supposed to have hair on his chest,"

her mother replied calmly. "Now go back up-stairs."

A few minutes later Ramona ran into the kitchen again. "Mama, he's got hair all over his legs!"

"He's-a supposed to, Ramona. Now go back upstairs like a good girl."

But when her groom took off his shoes and socks, Ramona saw that while one foot was normal, the other was a clubfoot. Faster than ever she raced down the stairs and yelled, "Mama, Mama, he's got half a foot."

"You stay here and cook the lasagna," said Mama, drying off her hands. "I'm-a going up-stairs."

•

One day Little Herbie heard a noise from his parents' room and opened the door to see them screwing. "What're you doing, Dad?" he asked.

"Just playing gin rummy with your mother," was the answer.

On the way back downstairs Little Herbie heard the same kind of noise coming from his grandparents room, opened the door, and asked what was going on. His grandad explained he was just playing gin rummy with his grandmother.

Not too much later dinner was served and everyone came to the table but Little Herbie. Looking in his room, Herbie's father found him lying on his bed, the sheets flapping up and down. "I'm just playing gin rummy," explained the boy.

"But you've got no one to play with," said his dad sternly.

"That's okay, Dad; with a hand like this, you don't need a partner."

•

The chief bosun's mate took advantage of any opportunity to bully the crew. When they returned to port it was time to paint the boat, and the mate had a fine time shouting down at the hapless sailors suspended over the side.

"Milligan," he bawled at one unfortunate, "you paint like I fuck!"

"I see, sir," said Milligan, looking up. "Did I get it on my face?"

•

A farmer realized his manhood was beginning to fail him, so he asked his doctor for a cure. The doctor gave him a small container of pills and told him to take no more than one a week. Back at the farm, the farmer thought he'd try the medication out on his stud horse first. The horse swallowed the pill, jumped out of his stall, kicked a side of the barn down and ran off down the road. "Those pills are too strong for me," the farmer figured, and he poured the rest into the well.

43

Later, when the doctor asked the farmer how the pills were working, the farmer said he had thrown them down the well. "Heavens!" the doctor exclaimed. "You haven't drank any of the water, have you?"

"Nope," answered the farmer. "We can't get the pump handle down."

•

What's a midget's circumcision?
A Tiny Trim.

•

One day when the teacher walked to the chalkboard, she noticed someone had written the word PENIS in tiny letters. She turned around and scanned the class looking for a guilty face. Finding none, she quickly erased it and began class.

The next day she went into the room and saw the word PENIS on the blackboard in somewhat larger letters. Again she looked around in vain for the culprit, so she proceeded with the day's lesson.

Every morning for about a week, she went into the classroom and found the word PENIS written on the board, each day's letters larger than the previous one's. Finally, just as she was growing accustomed to the prank, she walked in one day and instead found the words: "The more you rub it, the bigger it gets."

Did you hear about the butcher who got behind in his work?

He backed into the meat grinder.

•

Sam wants desperately to try to impress a beautiful lady customer. When she walks into his butcher shop one morning, he says, "Good morning, ma'am, and what can I do for you on this lovely day?"

Flashing him a no-nonsense look, the woman replies sternly, "Give me some of that prime rib that's on special."

Sam quickly shuffles around behind the counter. "It's been a long time since you've been by the shop," he says, the eagerness mounting in his voice, "so today I'll do something special for you: I won't put my thumb on the scale!"

To that, the pretty customer replies coldly, "Sam dear, if your dick were as big as that thumb, I'd buy my meat here all the time."

•

Explaining to his doctor that his sex life wasn't all it could be, Milt asked his doctor for a pill that would enable him to get it up for his wife. It so happened that the doctor had just the right medication, so Milt took a pill and drove home. But when he got to the apartment, his wife wasn't at home, and after waiting for an hour or so in growing discomfort, Milt finally had to jerk off.

When the doctor called to check in, Milt explained what had happened. "Well, gee, Milt, you didn't have to do for yourself," pointed out the doctor. "There are other women in the building."

"Doctor," said Milt, "for other women I don't need a pill."

•

A carpenter, an electrician, and a dentist had a mutual friend who was getting married, and in keeping with the custom, each was determined to play a practical joke on the newlyweds. The electrician decided to wire up the marriage bed so that when the two bodies touched, they'd get a shock. The carpenter planned to saw partly through the bed frame so that it would collapse when the shocked newlyweds jumped apart. And as the wedding approached, the dentist was still scratching his head and trying to come up with something.

After the honeymoon the new husband confronted his three friends. "I didn't mind too much when we got zapped," he told them, "and we both got a good laugh when the bed fell down. But who the hell put novocaine in the Vaseline?"

What's the definition of "dumb"?

A guy who rolls up his sleeve when a girl says she wants to feel his muscle.

•

A Scotsman stopped off for a few drinks at his local pub. On his way home he was having trouble navigating, so he decided to take a little rest by the roadside. As he was snoring gently, two girls came by and one said to the other, "You know, they say Scotsmen go naked under their kilts—shall we see if it's true?"

Her companion eagerly agreed, and when they lifted his kilt they found the story to be true indeed. In fact, what greeted their eyes was so pleasing that one of the girls took her blue hair ribbon and tied it around the man's dick as he slept.

Not too much later the Scotsman awoke, and when he stood up to take a pee he got quite a start at the sight of the blue ribbon. "Hoot man!" he exclaimed. "I don't know what you've been up to, but I'm certainly glad to see you took first place."

•

The patient cleared his throat a little embarrassedly before explaining his rather unusual problem. "YOU SEE, DOC," he boomed in a voice so deep and raspy it was almost impossible to understand, "I CAN'T GO ON WITH THIS VOICE ANYMORE—IT'S DRIVING ME CRAZY. CAN YOU FIX IT SO I SOUND LIKE A NORMAL PERSON?"

"I'll certainly try," said the doctor. After examining the patient, he reported that some sort of weight was pulling on the vocal cords and distorting the voice. "Any idea what it could be?" he queried.

The patient cleared his throat again. "ACTUALLY, DOC, I HAPPEN TO BE, UH, ESPECIALLY WELL-ENDOWED, AND MAYBE THAT'S WHAT'S DOING IT. LISTEN, IF YOU HAVE TO REMOVE SOME OF IT, THAT'S FINE BY ME. I'LL DO *ANYTHING* TO GET A VOICE LIKE A REGULAR GUY." So the doctor went ahead and performed the operation.

Two weeks later the patient telephoned the doctor's office. "Hey, listen," he babbled happily, "I can't thank you enough. Finally I sound like anyone else—it's just great!" After a pause, he asked, "Say, by the way, what'd you do with the piece of my penis you removed?"

"I THREW IT AWAY."

•

Why did the girl blow her lover after sex?
    She wanted to have her cock and eat it too.

•

One day Bobby's teacher tells the class they're going to play a thinking game, and asks for a volunteer. "Pick me, pick me," begs Bobby.

"Okay, Bobby," the teacher agrees. "Now I'm going to describe objects to you and you tell me what they are. Here we go: what's red, shiny, and you eat it?"

"A cherry," says Bobby.

"No, it's an apple, but it shows you're thinking," says the teacher gently. "Ready for the next one? What's yellow and you eat it?"

"A lemon," says Bobby.

"No," says the teacher, "it's a banana, but it shows you're thinking."

Before the teacher can continue, Bobby interrupts. "Okay, teacher, I've got one for you." He reaches into his pocket, looks down, pulls his hand out, and asks, "What's long, pink, and has a little red head on the end of it?"

"Oooh, Bobby!" squeals the teacher.

"No, it's a match—but it shows you're thinking."

•

NEW MALE HORROR MOVIE: Chainsaw Vasectomy.

•

One day this guy woke up to find that he had three bright red circles around the base of his penis. Panicked, he rushed to the doctor, thinking he'd contracted some new kind of herpes or VD. The doctor was equally puzzled by the symptoms, gave the guy a course of antibiotics, and told him to come back in a week if the rings didn't clear up.

A week later the guy was back in the doctor's office but the second dose of medication had no effect either. On his third visit the doctor told the guy to try various creams, soaps, and lotions. The next day the patient was back. "It worked, it worked!" he announced ecstatically.

"Oh really? And what did you use to get rid of the rings?" asked the doctor.

"Lipstick remover."

•

What does the perfect male look like?
   Long, dark, and handsome.

•

Three friends are out enjoying a night on the town, and the suggestion that they visit the local whorehouse meets with enthusiasm all around—especially when the madam tells them there's a special offer that evening. For $100, $150, or $200, the customer will receive a sexual treat beyond his wildest dreams.

The first guy forks out $100, is shown to the first door on the right, and soon his friends hear cries of ecstasy coming from within. He emerges sometime later, still sweaty and out of breath and grinning from ear to ear. "She's the most beautiful woman I've ever seen," he says happily, and goes on to explain that after extensive foreplay she had put two pineapple rings around his penis and eaten them.

The second guy can hardly wait to fork over his $150, is shown to a room, and soon wild cries of bliss can be heard. Eventually he returns with the same grin and the same story, except that he had gotten whipped cream along with the two pineapple rings.

The third guy needs little persuading to part with his $200 and is shown to an upstairs room. Soon cries of ecstasy can be heard, but his friends are puzzled when they're interrupted by a scream of agony. When he returns, they can't wait to hear what happened. Yes, he explains wearily, she was the most beautiful woman he'd ever seen, and after extensive foreplay she covered his prick with two pineapple rings, whipped cream, chopped nuts, and topped it off with a maraschino cherry.

"So then what happened?" ask his friends eagerly.

"Well," he replies, "it looked so good, I took a bite myself."

•

What's green and used to fry pricks?
  A Peter Pan.

What goes "Ha! Ha! Thump! Thump!"?

A man laughing his balls off.

•

There was this guy who desperately wanted to have sex with his girlfriend. However, he was too embarrassed because of his extremely small penis. So one night he took her to a dark place where she couldn't see it, and after furiously making out with her, dropped his pants and put his penis in her hand.

"Sorry, I don't smoke," she whispered.

•

At the doctor for an examination, this guy pulls down his pants to expose a penis the size of an olive. When the doctor and nurse crack up, the guy snaps, "Whatsa matter, never seen a hard-on before?"

•

One day a young woman was walking home when a man grabbed her, dragged her into a back alley, and started molesting her. "Help! Help me, someone," she cried. "I'm being robbed!"

"You ain't being robbed, lady," interrupted the man, "you're being screwed."

"Well, if this is being screwed," she retorted, "I'm being robbed."

•

Harry stopped by the funeral parlor to see his friend Joe, and found the embalmer at work on a corpse with a gigantic penis. The man's apparatus was so spectacular that Harry blurted out, "Wouldn't I love to have that cock!"

"You might as well—this guy doesn't need it anymore," said Joe, and he proceeded to cut off the organ and hand it over.

Harry wrapped it up carefully and took it home, where he found his wife in the kitchen making dinner. Deciding to have a little fun, Harry unwrapped the package, stuck it between his legs, and rushed into the kitchen, shouting, "Look, honey, look!"

His wife took one look and asked, "What happened to Sidney?"

•

What's a baby before it's born?
  Daddy's little squirt.

•

What do pitchers and gigolos have in common?
  Fast balls.

•

How do you quit masturbation?

Cold jerky.

•

A man who had problems with premature ejaculation went to a sex shop for a remedy. The clerk handed him a little yellow can and said, "This is Stay-Hard Spray; put on a little and you can go all night!"

Delighted, the guy took it home, stowed it on the cellar shelf, and waited eagerly for bedtime, when he sprayed some on his dick and went upstairs to his wife. But it seemed to make him come quicker than ever. The next day he returned to the sex shop, slammed the can down on the counter, and snapped, "This stuff makes me worse than before!"

Reading the label, the clerk asked, "Did you hide this stuff on the cellar shelf?"

"Yeah, so?" said the disgruntled customer.

"You must have grabbed the wrong can. This is Easy-Off."

•

Girl in music store: "Have you got Hot Lips on a ten-inch Decca?

Clerk: "No, but I've got hot nuts on a nine-inch pecker."

Girl: "Is that a record?"

Clerk: "No, but it's better than average."

What begins with F, ends in K, and can easily be replaced if it doesn't work?

A fork.

•

Did you hear about the new male-hygiene deodorant called Umpire?

It gets rid of foul balls.

•

Why is a bachelor skinny and a married man fat?

The bachelor comes home, sees what's in the refrigerator, and goes to bed; the married man comes home, sees what's in the bed, and goes to the refrigerator.

•

What do you do with 365 used rubbers?

Make them into a tire and call it a Goodyear.

•

"In return for releasing me from my imprisonment in that cursed bottle," said grateful Gina the Genie to Paul the Pauper, "I hereby grant you three wishes—however, your worst enemy will get twice what you do."

"Fine with me," agreed Paul. "For my first wish, I'd like to be rich beyond my wildest dreams." Immediately he was surrounded by caskets of precious stones, gold bullion, and negotiable securities.

"There you go," said Gina. "But your worst enemy now has a hoard that would put J. Paul Getty and all the Rockefellers to shame."

"That's okay. For my second wish, I'd like a harem of the world's most beautiful and alluring women, ready to fulfill my every desire." And—poof!—a bevy of beauties surrounded him, giggling and fluttering their eyelashes.

"But your worst enemy now has a harem that would put Sheik Yamani to shame," pointed out the genie.

"That's okay," said Paul, grinning. "For my third wish, I'd like *one* of my testicles to disappear."

•

Two very nervous young men got to talking in the doctor's waiting room and discovered they had similar symptoms: one had a red ring around the base of his penis and the other one a green ring. The fellow with the red ring was examined first. In a few minutes he came out, all smiles, and said, "Don't worry, man, it's nothing!"

Vastly relieved, the second patient went in to the examining room, only to be told a few minutes later by the doctor, "I'm very sorry, but you have an advanced case of VD and your penis will have to be amputated."

Turning white as a sheet, the young man gasped, "But the first guy . . . he said it was no big deal!"

"Well, you know," said the doctor, "there's a big difference between gangrene and lipstick."

•

What's the definition of a skyjacking?
A hand job at 33,000 feet.

•

Why do guys sleep better on their sides?
They have a kickstand.

•

Why do men shake their cocks after they piss?
Because they can't train them to go "SNIFF."

•

Three guys are walking down the street when they're suddenly stopped by a big black guy who jumps out in front of them. "You better have ten inches of dick between the three of you, or I might have to have some fun with my knife," he says, pulling out a switchblade.

The first guy coolly whips out his five-incher. The second guy isn't far behind with his fourincher, and the third produces his one-incher. Satisfied, the black guy lets them go.

The three head off around the corner, where the first guy gasps, "Good thing I had my five-incher."

The second guy says, "Yeah, and we're lucky I had my four inches."

"No kidding," says the third guy. "Thank God I had a hard-on!"

PART TWO:
FEMALE ANATOMY

Why's the new contraceptive sponge such a great idea?

Because after sex the woman can get up and wash the dishes.

•

It seems there was this woman who hated wearing underwear. One day she decided to go shopping for a new pair of shoes, and since she was wearing a skirt the salesman was enjoying an excellent view. After the third or fourth pair of shoes, the guy couldn't stand it anymore. "Lady," he said, "that's some beautiful sight. I could eat that pussy full of ice cream."

Disgusted, the woman ran out of the store and went home. When her husband got home from work she told him about the incident and asked him to go beat the shit out of the salesman. And when he flatly refused, she wanted to know why.

"Three reasons," said her husband. "Number one: you shouldn't have been out in a skirt with no underpants. Number two: you have enough shoes to last you ten more years. And number three: any son of a bitch who can eat that much ice cream I don't want to fuck with in the first place."

•

What are the three best things about being a woman?

You can bleed without cutting yourself;

You can bury a bone without digging a hole;

And you can make a man come without calling him.

•

What's a female Taurus?

A Clitaurus, of course.

•

If God made the top half of a woman, who made the bottom?

A black. Who else would give it big lips, kinky hair, and a smell like a catfish?

Three women decided to share an apartment, and by coincidence they all had boyfriends named Leroy. After a week things got so confusing that they decided to give each man a nickname from a brand of soda. The first woman said, "I'll name mine Mountain Dew, because he lives on a mountain and he loves to do, do do!"

"I'll name mine 7-Up," said the second, "because he's seven inches long and he's always up."

The third woman thought for a while, then said, "I'll name mine Jack Daniels."

"That's not a soda," pointed out her roommates, "that's a liquor."

She smiled. "That's my Leroy."

•

Mabel had tried every diet plan in the world to no avail, and finally had to agree that some sort of daily exercise was required if she was going to lose weight. Her doctor suggested a program of calisthenics, so Mabel dutifully started "bicycling" with her feet in the air, only to find that her pants were so tight that she couldn't complete the exercise. So Mabel decided to try it in the nude, but o-o-o-h, those rug burns. Finally she tried doing the exercise on her bed, and it worked fine.

Unfortunately a few days into the program,

Mabel threw her legs over her head so energetically that they got caught in her wrought-iron headboard. Mabel was well and truly stuck, and could do nothing but moan for help until her husband got home from work. Hearing her feeble groans, he sauntered into the bedroom, only to exclaim, "Why, Mabel, if you'd put your teeth in and comb your hair, you'd look just like your mother!"

•

A hooker went into the bank to put away some newly-acquired earrings. "I happen to know something about jewelry, Madam," confided the teller, "and I hope you know that these are not genuine diamonds."

"Oh my God!" screamed the hooker. "I've been raped!"

•

A woman went to apply for a job as a truck driver. Not too keen on the idea, the personnel manager for the trucking company pointed out, "You have to be pretty tough to cut it as a truck driver, you know."

"I'm tough, I really am," said the eager applicant.

"Well, do you drink and smoke?"

"Yes, of course."

"Do you cuss a lot?" asked the interviewer.

"You bet," said the woman. "I cuss like a lumberjack."

"So have you ever been picked up by the fuzz?"

"Well, no," she admitted, "but I've been swung around by the tits a couple of times."

•

What's better than a cold Budweiser?

A warm Busch.

•

This guy screwed a hooker and spent his last dime on her. Only at the end did he realize he was penniless, so he asked if he could borrow the dime so he get home on the bus. "Sure," she said, "if you eat it out of my twat."

So the man got down on his hands and knees and went to work, and after a few minutes he said, "I got it. See ya." A little while later his bus pulled up, and he dropped it in the token box and sat down.

The bus driver turned around and hollered, "Hey buddy, how far do you think you're going to get on that scab?"

•

Did you hear the new slogan for Clairol hair color?

"Buy a double batch and get a snatch to match!"

•

Did you hear about the prostitute with a degree in psychology?

She'll blow your mind.

•

The gynecologist stuck up his head after completing his examination. "I'm sorry, Miss," he said, "but removing that vibrator is going to involve a very lengthy and delicate operation."

"I'm not sure I can afford it," sighed the young woman on the examining table. "Why don't you just replace the batteries?"

•

One night Jerry brought home a dozen roses to his wife. "How lovely, dear," she commented. "What's the occasion?"

"I want to make love to you," he said simply.

"Not tonight, dear. I have a headache."

The next night Jerry came home with a big box of chocolates and explained that he wanted to make love.

"I'm awfully tired, honey," said his wife. "Not tonight."

Every night for a week Jerry brought home an elegant gift, but each time his wife's answer was no. Finally he came home with six black kittens with little red bows around their necks and handed them to his wife. "How adorable, Jerry," she exclaimed. "But what are they for?"

"These are six little pallbearers for your dead pussy."

•

One night little Johnny walked in on his parents while they were screwing. "Daddy," he cried, "what are you and Mommy doing?"

"Uh . . . we're making a little sister for you to play with," stammered his father.

"Oh, neat," said Johnny, and went back to bed.

The next day his dad came home to find the little boy sobbing his eyes out on the front porch. "What's wrong, Johnny?" he asked, picking him up.

"You know the little sister you and Mommy made me?"

"Yes," said his father, blushing.

The little boy wailed, "Today the milkman ate it!"

•

What giggles and smokes like a chimney?

A white woman in heat.

•

Rick was trying real hard to get the best-looking cheerleader in school to go out on a date with him. She finally agreed, but only on condition that he arrange a date for her best friend, too. That was fine with Rick—but when Friday night came around he hadn't been able to line anyone up, so he asked his retarded brother Bill to help him out. "Why, sure," said Bill. "But you know, I've never been out with a girl before."

"No problem," said Rick. "Just do everything I do."

Off the four of them went to the drive-in, and when Rick started kissing his date, Bill followed suit. Soon Rick had the cheerleader's bra undone, so Rick undid his date's. Next, Rick started feeling inside her panties, but when Bill tried to follow suit, his date told him to quit.

"Why?" asked Bill, anxiously noting that his brother was getting quite a head start in the back seat.

"I have my period," she said.

"You're what?"

"I'm bleeding down there," she explained, blushing.

"This I gotta see," said Bill. He turned on the headlights, dragged his date out in front of the car, pulled down her pants, and yelled, "Hell, I'd be bleeding too if my dick was chopped off!"

•

Who are the six most important men in a woman's life?

The doctor: he says, "Take your clothes off."

The dentist: he says, "Open wide."

The hairdresser: he says, "Do you want it teased or blown?"

The interior decorator: he says, "You'll like it once it's in."

The milkman: he says, "Do you want it in front or in back?"

The banker: he says, "If you take it out, you'll lose interest."

•

This guy is out on a date with a girl and they end up back at his apartment on the couch with the lights off. Suddenly, to his horror, his hairpiece falls off, and he begins to grope around in the dark for it.

Not realizing what's happened, his date starts cooing passionately. "That's it, honey," she whispers, "right there. You've got it . . . you've got it now. . . ."

"No I don't," he says, sitting up and looking at her. "My hairpiece isn't parted in the middle."

•

Hear about the woman who was so ugly that when she was born, the doctor slapped her mother?

•

There's this whore who gets all gussied up every Saturday night, makes the rounds of the bars, and says she'll give any man five hundred dollars if he can make a rhyme to rhyme with hers:

> "Three plus three is six
> Six plus three is nine
> I can guess the length of yours
> But you can't guess the depth
> of mine."

She does this for about a month and nobody can match her rhyme. So late one Saturday night she's walking home alone when she comes across a drunk. She makes him the same offer, and after scratching his head and thinking for a minute, the guy says, "I got it:

> Three plus three may be six
> And six plus three may be nine
> I bet you I can piss in yours
> But you can't piss in mine!"

•

A well-built guy and his gorgeous date came out of the movie theater and strolled down to the neighborhood coffeehouse. As they stepped inside, each of the regulars swiveled around on their seats to check out the newcomers and then turned back to their conversations—with one notable exception. This one fellow was ogling the woman with bulging eyes and tongue hanging out, practically drooling on his shirt-front.

Enraged by this crude behavior, the woman's

date walked over, grabbed the offender by his shirt collar, and shook him like a dishrag. "I'll teach you to stare at my woman with those filthy thoughts written all over your ugly face," he bellowed. "Any more ideas like that come into your head and I'll slice you up like salami —is that clear?"

"Oh, absolutely, sir," quavered the terrified fellow. "I truly meant no offense. I assure you I wasn't entertaining any sort of impure thoughts, just admiring your taste in female companionship."

Somewhat mollified, the man slowly released his grip on the shirt collar.

Straightening his shirt, the voyeur went on in a more confident tone of voice, "In fact if you'd care to have a seat, I'd be delighted to buy you both a cup of pussy."

•

What do you get when you cross a stripper and a fruit?

A banana that peels itself.

•

How about when you cross an elephant and a prostitute?

A hooker who does it for peanuts and won't ever forget you.

•

71

What does a cow have four of and a woman have two of?

Feet.

•

A young couple hadn't been married for long when, one morning, the man came up behind his wife as she got out of the shower and grabbed her by the buttocks. "Y'know, honey," he said smugly, "if you firmed these up a little bit, you wouldn't have to keep using your girdle."

Her feelings were so hurt that she refused to speak to him for the rest of the day.

Only a week later he again stepped into the bathroom just as she was drying off from her shower. Grabbing both breasts, he said, "Y'know, honey, if you firmed these up a bit, you wouldn't have to keep wearing a bra."

The young wife was infuriated, but waited till the next morning to exact her revenge. When her husband stepped out of the shower, she grabbed him by the penis and hissed, "Y'know, honey, if you firmed this up a little bit, I wouldn't have to keep using your brother."

•

What does a woman say after her third orgasm?

You mean you don't know?

•

You know God wouldn't have made women smell like fish . . .

. . . if He hadn't made come look like tartar sauce.

•

An elegant woman swathed in furs entered a very expensive pharmacy in her neighborhood. Coming up to a white-gowned employee, she asked him where batteries for her vibrator could be located.

The young man thought for a moment, then turned toward the rear of the store, saying politely, "Come with me."

"If I could come that way," spat the dowager, "I wouldn't need the batteries."

•

"The man next to me is jerking off!" hissed Irene to her girlfriend as they sat in the darkened movie theater.

"Just ignore him" was her friend's advice.

"I can't," moaned Irene. "He's using my hand."

•

What happens when a girl puts her panties on backwards?

She gets her ass chewed out.

•

The young lady was wearing an extremely tight skirt, and when she tried to board the Fifth Avenue bus she found she couldn't lift her leg high enough to reach the step. She reached back to undo her zipper a bit, but it didn't seem to do any good, so she reached back and unzipped it again.

Suddenly the man behind her lifted her up and placed her on the top step.

"How dare you!" she demanded, turning to face him.

"Well, lady," he replied, "by the time you unzipped my fly for the second time I figured we were good friends."

•

What do you call two women in the freezer?
Cold cunts.

•

What's the definition of an overbite?
When you're eating pussy and it tastes like shit.

•

What do you give a robot who's having her period?
An S.O.S. pad.

•

A woman goes into a bar and sits down. The bartender asks what she'd like to drink and she says, "Bring me a beer."

"Anheuser Busch?" asks the bartender.

"Just fine, thanks," she answers, "and how's your cock?"

•

What do a woman and a stamp have in common?

You can lick 'em, stick 'em, and send 'em away.

•

"Say," began Lucille one day over lunch, "weren't you going to go out with that guy who played the French horn?"

"Yeah," said Diane, stirring her iced tea.

"You were really looking forward to it, I remember. How'd it go?" Lucille leaned forward eagerly.

"Actually he was a pretty nice guy," volunteered Diane reluctantly. "But there was one real problem . . ."

"Oh, really?"

"Every time he kissed me, he wanted to shove his fist up my ass."

•

What did the Florida entrepreneur name his whorehouse?

Bush Gardens.

•

Why did God create the orgasm?

Because He couldn't wait for the second coming.

•

A certain couple fell on really hard times, and since the husband already worked full-time and part of a night shift, they decided the only way to keep the family afloat was for the wife to go out and sell her body.

One night she didn't return until the wee hours, disheveled and exhausted. Watching her flop onto the sofa like a limp dishrag, her husband said sympathetically, "You look like you've really had a rough night, honey."

"I sure have," she gasped.

"Well, did you make a lot of money, at least?" he asked.

His wife managed a proud smile. "One hundred and thirty dollars and fifty cents."

"Fifty cents!" exclaimed the husband. "Who was the cheap bastard who only gave you four bits?"

"Why," she explained, *"all* of them."

•

Why did the hooker wear French heels?
She didn't want to sell herself short.

•

"That was . . . terrific. Really amazing!" gasped the new boyfriend gratefully.

"I'm glad you liked it," said the girl demurely. "I learned it in the circus."

"No kidding? How's that?"

"I was a sword swallower."

•

The newlyweds undressed and got into bed. "Sweetheart," asked the new wife, "could you please hand me that jar of Vaseline over there?"

"Baby, you aren't going to need any Vaseline," he growled amorously. But at her insistence he handed it over, and she proceeded to smear it liberally all over her crotch.

After watching this procedure, the husband asked the wife a favor. "Remember that long string of pearls I gave you for an engagement present? Could you get them out of the bureau drawer for me?"

"Of course, lover," replied his bride. "But whatever do you want them for?"

"Well," he explained, looking down at the Vaseline smeared all over her, "if you think I'm going into a mess like that without chains, you're crazy!"

•

"I do happen to need somebody," admitted the owner of the hardware store to the unimpressive-looking man who was interested in a job. "But tell me, can you sell?"

"Of course," was the confident reply.

"I mean really *sell*," reiterated the shopkeeper.

"You bet," answered the young man.

"I'll show you what I mean," said the owner, going over to a customer who had just walked in and asked for grass seed. "We're having a very special sale on lawn mowers," he told the customer. "Could I interest you in one?"

"What do I need a lawn mower for?" protested the customer. "I don't even have any grass yet."

"Maybe not," said the owner agreeably, "but all that seed's going to grow like crazy someday, and then you'll need a lawn mower in the worst way. And you won't find them on sale in midsummer, that's for sure."

"I guess you've got a point," admitted the fellow. "Okay, I'll take a lawn mower, too."

"Think you can do that?" the storekeeper, writing up the bill, asked his new employee. The man nodded. "Okay, good. Now I have to run to the bank. I'll only be gone for a few minutes, but while I'm gone I want you to sell, sell, sell."

The new guy's first customer was a woman

who came over and asked where the tampons were.

"Third aisle over, middle of the second shelf."

When she came to the counter to pay, he leaned over and said, "Hey, you wanna buy a lawn mower? They're on sale."

"Why on earth would I want a lawn mower?" she asked, eyeing him suspiciously.

"Well, you aren't going to be fucking," he blurted, "so you might as well mow the lawn."

•

With one look at his voluptuous new patient, all the gynecologist's professional ethics went right out the window. Instructing her to undress completely, he began to stroke the soft skin of her inner thigh. "Do you know what I'm doing?" he asked softly.

"Checking for any dermatological abnormalities, right?"

"Right," crooned the doctor, beginning to fondle her breasts and gently pinch her nipples. "And now?"

"Looking for any lumps that might be cancerous."

"Right you are," reassured the doctor, placing her feet in the stirrups, pulling out his cock, and entering her. "And do you know what I'm doing now?"

"Yup," she said, looking down. "Catching herpes."

Define cunt:
  A root canal.

·

What's a prostitute's favorite rock group?
  "Yes."

·

What's black and hairy and fell off the wall?
  Humpty Cunt!

·

A famous Soviet ballerina defected to the U.S., so there was considerable excitement on the opening night of her American premiere. Everything went along very smoothly before a very receptive audience, and finally it was time for the grand finale. The entire troupe swirled about the ballerina, who performed a final spectacular set of leaps and landed in a perfect split in center stage.

Needless to say, the crowd went wild, and it was only after a standing ovation and five curtain calls that the curtain closed for the last time. Rushing onstage to the ballerina, who was still holding the perfect split, the director began to congratulate her on her superb performance.

"Performance, hell," hissed the dancer. "Rock me back and forth to break the seal."

•

Leonard desperately wanted to become a doctor and had really crammed for his medical boards, so he wasn't in the least fazed by the question: "Name the three advantages of breast milk."

Quickly he wrote, "1) It contains the optimum balance of nutrients for the newborn child." He added, "2) As it is contained within the mother's body, it is protected from germs and helps develop the child's immune system."

Then Leonard was stumped. Sitting back and racking his brains until he'd broken into a sweat, he finally scribbled, "3) It comes in such nice containers."

•

Two law partners can't resist hiring a gorgeous young receptionist, and despite promises to the contrary, neither can resist going to bed with her. And not too long afterwards their worst fears are realized: the blushing receptionist announces that she's pregnant. No one knows who the father is, and the partners are in a total quandary. So toward the end of the pregnancy they decide to chip in and send the girl off to Florida to have the baby.

Several months go by with no news, and finally one of the partners feels so guilty that he hops on a flight to Miami to check on the young mother. The next night the phone rings in their New York office.

"How is she?" asks his partner.

"Oh, she's fine," is the breezy answer, "but I've got some bad news and some good news."

"Oh yeah? What's the good news?"

"Well, like I said, Jeannette's fine. And she had twins."

"So what's the bad news?" asked the partner from New York.

"Mine died."

•

If whiskey makes you frisky and gin makes you grin, what makes you pregnant?

Two highballs and a squirt.

•

The voluptuous stewardess asked the dirty old man, "May I offer you some TWA soda, some TWA coffee, or some TWA milk?"

Winking lewdly, he suggested, "How about some TWA tea?"

•

The job of assistant at the general store had been taken over by a ripe but none too bright young girl with a penchant for short skirts. The local boys delighted in sending her on errands to the top shelves of the store because the view from underneath the ladder was most enticing.

One morning, noticing that all the raisin bread was stocked on an upper shelf, the guys were amusing themselves by sending the girl up the ladder again and again. An older man walked into the store and waited in line, quietly taking in the scene. Returning behind the counter with the last loaf of bread under her arm, she asked him, "Is yours raisin too?"

"No," he admitted, "but it's starting to twitch."

•

What do electric train sets and women's breasts have in common?

Both were intended for children, but it's the fathers who play with them.

•

What's harder than getting six pregnant women in a Volkswagen?

Getting six women pregnant in a Volkswagen.

•

The conductor was hard at work on his podium when he heard severe disharmony from the cello section. Stopping the orchestra, he glared at the lady cellist.

"My dear madam," he snapped, "you have a

magnificent instrument between your legs. Must you stand there and simply scratch at it?"

•

Did you hear about the call-girl who accidentally made two appointments at the same time?
    She managed to squeeze both of them in.

•

What do you call a man and a woman using the rhythm method of birth control?
    Parents.

•

What's a rib-tickler?
    A vibrator shoved in too far.

•

[You need to be holding something to drink when you tell this one.]
    Knowing her fiancé was also a virgin, the night before the wedding the bride-to-be asked her mother about the mysteries of sex. Her mother was glad to oblige with some pointers.
    That night, following all the festivities, the nervous husband took off his glasses and slid under the covers, but just looking at his pretty new wife gave him a massive hard-on. "I think I know what to do," she said, sizing up the situation, and proceeded to go down on him. After

just a minute or two the fellow couldn't contain himself and blew his wad. As he raved about how fantastic it had felt, his wife got into her side of the bed, but almost immediately felt another hard-on against her thigh. Looking over at him, she proceeded to go down on him again. And, groaning with ecstasy, the husband blew his wad again.

"Oh, darling," he said, getting to his hands and knees beside the bed, "you've pleased me so very much. Is there anything I can do for you?"

[Now's when you ask, "What do you think she said?" and take a swallow in your mouth.]

"Kiss me." [Spit out your drink.]

•

What's the definition of eternity?

The length of time between when *you* come and *she* leaves.

•

John: "Did you hear that report on the six-o'clock news about the old lady found with a rat in her stomach?"
Ray: "No. How'd it happen?
John: "Her pussy fell asleep."

•

A female midget went to her gynecologist with the complaint that her crotch was hurting her.

"When does the pain occur?" he asked.

"When it's raining out, oddly enough," answered the patient.

"Since I don't see anything amiss, why don't you come in the next time it hurts?" proposed the doctor.

The very next rainy day the midget limped into his office. "Doc, my crotch is killing me right now."

The doctor had her lie on the table in the examining room and put her feet in the stirrups. Covering her knees with a sheet, he reached for some surgical scissors and began to snip away. "That should do it," he reported, sticking his head up after a few minutes.

Dressing and coming into his office, the woman exclaimed, "Doctor, the pain is completely gone! How did you do it?"

The doctor explained modestly, "Oh, I just cut two inches off the tops of your galoshes."

•

The new stewardess was summoned to the office of the head of the training program for a severe reprimand. "I heard about that episode on your first flight, Miss Larson," said the director, glaring over the top of her glasses. "From now on, whenever a passenger feels faint, I'll thank you to push his head down between his own legs!"

•

As the woman in front of him stepped up into the bus, the man noticed that her skirt was stuck between the cheeks of her ass, so he reached up and pulled it free.

"How dare you!" yelped the woman, turning and slapping him in the face.

"Sorry, lady," said the man, and stuck it back in again.

•

Sam and Cindy grew up next door to each other, and as they grew older each constantly tried to one-up the other. If Sam got a jungle gym, Cindy got a swing set, and so on, until the contest became a very expensive one for both sets of parents. Finally Sam's father asked what was going on, and when Sam explained it, a big grin came over his dad's face.

Next Saturday Cindy whizzed down the sidewalk on a brand new tricycle. "Nyaah, nyaah," she taunted, "look what I've got."

"So?" retorted Sam. "I've got something you'll never have—look!" And he pulled down his pants and showed her.

Realizing she'd been outdone, Cindy ran into her house sobbing. Her father picked her up and tried to comfort her. Getting the whole story out of her, he smiled and whispered something in her ear.

The next day Sam spotted Cindy in the backyard and decided to rub it in. "I've got one of these and you don't," he teased, pulling his pants down again.

"Big deal," said Cindy haughtily, pulling her skirt up and her underpants down. "My Daddy says that with one of *these* I can have as many of *those* as I want."

•

What was Adam's first toy?

Eve.

•

After Marty's and Mindy's marriage ended in a particularly bitter divorce, Mindy remarried within six months. Not long afterwards she ran into her ex-husband at a local restaurant where she was having lunch with a girlfriend.

"So," said Marty, sidling up to their table, "how's your new husband?"

"Just fine, thanks," answered Mindy calmly.

"And how does he like your old, tired, worn-out pussy?" inquired Marty with a leer.

"Oh, he likes it just fine," Mindy said cheerfully, ". . . once he got past the old, worn-out part."

•

Drunk: "Knock, knock."
Woman: "Who's there?"
Drunk: "Emerson."

Woman: "Emerson who?"
Drunk: "Emerson pretty big tits you got there!"

•

What would be one of the best things about electing a woman for vice-president?
We wouldn't have to pay her as much!

•

What do a hooker and a shotgun have in common?
One cock and they're ready to blow.

•

What do a hooker and a doorknob have in common?
Everybody gets a turn.

•

What do a hooker and a pie have in common?
Everybody gets a piece.

•

What do a hooker and railroad tracks have in common?
They're spread all over.

•

What do a hooker and an ice cream cone have in common?

Everybody gets a lick.

•

What do a hooker and a bus have in common?

Everybody pays to get on.

•

The night watchman at a fancy funeral home was intrigued by the sight of a cork protruding from the vagina of a female corpse. Unable to resist temptation, he pulled out the cork, and nearly jumped out of his skin when "Moon River" started playing. Quickly he popped the cork back in, stopping the music. Unable to believe his ears, he pulled the cork a second time and out came the familiar melody.

At that the incredulous watchman ran to the phone to call his boss. "You aren't going to believe this," he shouted into the receiver. "You gotta come over to the home right now." When the disgruntled undertaker arrived, the night watchman dragged him over to the corpse, pulled out the cork, and out came "Moon River" as clear as a bell.

The undertaker grabbed the man by the shoulders and screamed, "You dragged me out of bed at three in the morning just to hear some cunt sing 'Moon River'?"

What's a nymphomaniac's dilemma?

Meeting a guy with a herpes and a huge prick.

•

One day Herb was in the mood for ice cream, so he walked to the nearby Baskin-Robbins and ordered a sundae. "And be sure to put a cherry on top," he instructed the waitress.

Fifteen minutes later the sundae arrived at his table. Pushing it away, Herb complained, "Where's the cherry? I'm not eating this."

Lifting her skirt, the waitress picked up the dish and sat on it. "Will this do?" she giggled.

"Well, okay," said Herb grudgingly, "but it better not have any stones in it or I'm not paying."

•

What's the best defense against rape?

Beating off the attacker.

•

What are "brownie points"?

What you find in a future girl scout's bra.

•

The night before her wedding Maria pulled her mother aside for an intimate little chat.

"Mom," she confided, "I want you to tell me how I can make my new husband happy."

The bride's mother took a deep breath. "Well, my child," she began, "when two people love, honor, and respect each other, love can be a very beautiful thing . . ."

"I know how to fuck, Mom," interrupted the girl. "I want you to teach me how to make lasagna."

•

What's a clitoris?

A female hood ornament.

•

Hilary had tried every diet in the world but still weighed in at a hefty 320 pounds. Finally she gave up, so depressed that she decided to kill herself, and she went out and bought a gun. The only problem was that she was unsure as to the exact location of her heart, so she called her doctor to ask.

"It's directly below your left breast," was the doctor's answer.

So Hilary hung up the phone and shot herself in the knee.

•

What's six inches long, has a bald head on it, and drives women crazy?

A one hundred dollar bill.

How do you make a hormone?
Don't pay her.

•

Who enjoys sex more, the man or the woman?
The woman.
How can I prove it?
When your ear itches and you put your little finger in and wiggle it around and take it out again, what feels better, your finger or your ear?

•

Three morticians were shooting the breeze at an undertaker's conference and the subject came around to what each considered his greatest achievement. Harry cleared his throat modestly and revealed that he had once had to deal with the remains of a man who had stepped on a hand grenade. "It took me three days," he said proudly, "but it was an open-casket funeral."

"Not bad," conceded Jerry, "but listen to this: I got handed a construction worker who'd been run over by a steamroller, and he was ready for that open casket in two days."

"You guys got me beat," sighed Charlie. "My toughest case was a lady parachutist who landed right on the Empire State Building. It took me four days just to get the grin off her face."

•

How do Valley Girls part their hair?
   In the middle. [Spread your legs.]

•

Hear about the nympho who went to the beach?
   She was asked to leave the area after the lifeguard caught her going down for the third time.

•

Susie was desperate for her new husband to go down on her. After everything from subtle innuendo to outright begging had failed, she finally resorted to trickery. "Honey," she called breathily from the bedroom one night, "can you help me a sec? I've got a tampon stuck inside me. I'm sure you can get it out if you use your teeth."
   Disgusted, the husband pulled the diamond engagement ring off her finger and pushed it way up inside her.
   "Owww!" yelped the young bride. "What did you do *that* for?"
   "You really expect me to go poking around down there," snarled her husband, "for a lousy tampon?"

Why do women have two sets of lips?
  So they can piss and moan at the same time.

•

What's white and black and red all over?
  A half-breed on the rag.

•

During his many years in the Merchant
Marine, Ernie had really gotten around, so
when he got shore leave in Bangkok, he asked
the madam of the whorehouse for something
exotic.

"I have just the thing," offered the madam,
not in the least nonplussed. "Cyclops Susie."

Out from the beaded curtain behind the desk
came a girl with one glass eye. As soon as she
and Ernie were alone together, Susie popped
out the eye, presented him with the socket, and
urged him to go at it. Ernie swallowed nervously but obeyed, and when it was over he was
delirious with ecstasy. "That was the best I've
ever had. Unbelievable! God, I can hardly wait
till I'm back in Bangkok," he gushed to the
hooker.

"Don't worry, honey," said Susie graciously.
"I'll keep an eye out for you."

•

What do you call pulling off a girl's pantyhose?
  Foreplay.

•

Three women arrived simultaneously at the gates of Heaven and were greeted by St. Peter. "There will be a place for each of you once you have confessed your sins," he assured them, turning gravely to the first woman.

"I married one man but I loved another," she admitted, blushing, "so I divorced my husband and married the man I loved."

"Show her to the silver gates," St. Peter instructed a minion, and turned to the second woman.

"I loved one man, married him, and lived happily ever after," went her story. St. Peter directed her to be shown through the golden gates, and turned toward the third woman.

"I was a dancer in a cabaret," she confessed with a becoming blush, "and I pleased every man who came to see me, pleased them well for the right price."

"Show her to my room" said St. Peter.

•

A fellow met this girl, and she seemed willing and he was dying to try, so even though they didn't know quite what to do, very soon they were doing it. "If I'd known you were a virgin," the man said afterwards, "I'd have taken my time."

"If I'd known you had time," she retorted, "I'd have taken off my pantyhose."

•

Little Molly was taken to the beauty parlor for her first haircut. The strange surroundings intimidated her and she began to cry, but the hairdresser was used to children and calmly offered her a cookie. Sure enough, the little girl quieted down so he began cutting her hair, but in only a few minutes Molly started up again.

"What's the matter, little girl?" asked the hairdresser solicitously. "Have you gotten hair on your cookie?"

"What are you, a pervert?" she snapped. "I'm only six!"

•

How can you pick out a paranoid woman?

She's the one putting a condom on her vibrator.

•

What do spaghetti and women have in common?

They both wiggle when you eat them.

•

An amateur golfer playing in his first tournament was delighted when a beautiful girl came up to him after the round and suggested he come over to her place for the night. The fellow was a bit embarrassed to explain that he really couldn't stay all night but that he'd be glad to come over for a while. Twenty minutes later they were in her bed making love. And when it was over, he got out of bed and started getting dressed.

"Hey," called the girl from beneath the covers, "where do you think you're going? Arnold Palmer wouldn't leave so early."

At that the golfer stripped off his clothes and jumped back on top of her. Once they'd made love a second time, he got out of bed and put his pants back on.

"What're are you up to?" she called. "Jack Nicklaus wouldn't think of leaving now." So the golfer pulled off his pants and screwed her a third time, and afterwards he started getting dressed.

"C'mon, you can't leave yet," protested the girl. "Lee Trevino wouldn't call it a day."

"Lady, would you tell me one thing?" asked the golfer, looking at her very seriously. "What's par for this hole?"

•

The first astronaut to land on Mars was delighted to come across a beautiful Martian woman stirring a huge pot over a campfire. "Hi there," he said casually. "What're you doing?"

"Making babies," she explained, looking up with a winsome smile.

Horny after the long space voyage, the astronaut decided to give it a shot. "That's not the way we do it on Earth," he informed her.

"Oh, really? And how is it done on your planet?"

"Well, it's kind of hard to describe," he conceded, "but I'd be glad to show you."

"Fine," agreed the lovely Martian maiden, and the two proceeded to make love in the glow of the fire. When they were finished, she asked, "So where are the babies?"

"Oh, they don't show up for another nine months," explained the astronaut patiently.

"So why'd you stop stirring?"

•

Definition of henpecked:

A sterile husband afraid to tell his pregnant wife.

•

What do you call a female peacock?

A peacunt.

•

A well-endowed woman entered a chic Madison Avenue boutique and tried on every evening gown in the store. Finally setting eyes on a very sexy, low-cut dress hanging in the display window, she asked the exhausted sales clerk if she could try it on.

"Of course, madam," he muttered through clenched teeth, squeezed into the window, and began the painstaking task of taking the dummy apart to remove the gown. Eventually he succeeded and was able to hand it over to the demanding customer.

"How do I look?" she asked, emerging from the dressing room. "Does it show off my marvelous breasts to advantage?"

"Oh, absolutely," the clerk assured her. "But do hairy chests run in your family?"

•

What should a woman give the man who has everything?

Encouragement.

•

The manager of a large lumberyard was approached by an elderly blind man looking for employment. "Sorry, pal," he said apologetically, "but you'd have to be able to identify all the different sorts of woods we carry, and frankly with your handicap—"

"No problem, young man, no problem at all," interrupted the blind man cheerfully. "I happen to know a great deal about lumber, and my sense of smell is exceedingly keen. Just give me a chance."

Utterly disbelieving, the foreman nonetheless led the old geezer over to a stack of two-by-fours. After a quick sniff, the blind man identified it as pine paneling.

"Right you are," conceded the manager, "but that's an easy one. How about this?" The blind man identified the next piece of wood as oak flooring, the next as birch veneer, then kiln-dried redwood. Flabbergasted, the manager thought of one last test. Instead of a piece of wood, he had his nude secretary brought out and held just beneath the old man's nose. "Well?" he demanded.

"This one's tough," admitted the blind man. "Could you flip it over for me?"

After a few more deep sniffs a big smile broke out on his wrinkled old face. "You tried to put one over on an old blind fellow, but it didn't work," he announced triumphantly. "You can't trick this nose of mine, no sirree. This here piece of wood's the shithouse door off a tuna boat!"

•

How did Helen Keller discover masturbation?
    Trying to read her own lips.

•

So why does she masturbate with just one hand?

So she can moan with the other.

•

Adam and Eve were strolling in the Garden of Eden after dinner one evening when Eve turned anxiously to her mate. "Adam," she asked, "tell me the truth. Do you love me?"

Adam shrugged. "Who else?"

•

After a few years of marriage the young woman became increasingly disturbed by her diminishing sex life. She tried everything she could think of on her husband, from greeting him at the door dressed in Saran Wrap to purchasing exotic paraphernalia from a mail-order sex boutique, but none of it had the desired effect on his libido, and finally she persuaded him to consult a hypnotist.

She was delighted that after only a few visits, her husband's ardor was restored to honeymoon dimensions. There was only one annoying side effect: every so often during lovemaking he would jump up and run out of the room for a minute or two. At first his wife didn't want to rock the boat, but eventually her curiosity overcame her better judgement. Following him into the bathroom, she saw him staring into the mirror, muttering, "She's not my wife. . . . She's not my wife. . . . She's not my wife. . . ."

•

Why didn't the Polish woman wear tight pants on her trip to Australia?

She was afraid of starting a bushfire.

•

What do you call a female Mexican with no legs?

Cuntsuelo.

•

Bert couldn't help noticing that his wife had been increasingly preoccupied and grouchy of late, but he wasn't inclined to do much about it until she leaned across the breakfast table one morning and slapped him hard.

"What the hell's that for?" he shouted, rubbing his cheek.

"That's for being such a lousy lover," she retorted, and stomped off into the kitchen. Bert lost no time in following her over to the sink, where he kicked her so hard she fell on the floor.

"Damn you, you schmuck," she cried. "Why'd you do that?"

"That," he explained, "is for knowing the difference."

•

Soon after their honeymoon, the young couple found themselves at the doctor's office, where each complained of exhaustion and fatigue. After examining them thoroughly, the doctor reassured them that there was no organic reason for their complaints.

"However, it's not at all uncommon for young people to wear themselves out in the first weeks or months of married life," he told them reassuringly. "What you both need is rest. For the next month, confine your sexual activity to those days of the week with an 'r' in them. That's Thursday, Friday, and Saturday," he went on with a wink, "and you'll be feeling up to snuff very soon."

Since the end of the week was approaching, the couple had no problem following the doctor's advice. But on the first scheduled night off, the new bride found herself increasingly restless and horny. Tossing and turning into the wee hours, she finally turned to her husband and shook him awake.

Groggy and bewildered, he mumbled, "What's wrong, baby? What day is it?"

"Mondray," she murmured.

•

As he got into bed the husband was very much in the mood, but was hardly surprised when his wife pushed his hand off her breast. "Lay off, honey. I have a headache."

"Perfect," he said without missing a beat. "I was just in the bathroom powdering my dick with aspirin."

•

What do you get when you cross a hooker with a Chinaman?

Someone who'll suck your laundry clean.

•

And when you cross a hooker with a JAP?

Someone who'll suck your credit cards.

•

What happens to Egyptian girls who forget to take their Pills?

They become mummies.

•

Three newly-pregnant women were in the waiting room at the obstetrician's office and they got to talking. "I was on top the night we conceived," confided one of the women, "and Doctor Friedman says we're going to have a girl."

"Is that so?" commented the second woman. "We did it missionary style, and Doctor Friedman assured me it's going to be a boy."

"Oh, shit," groaned the third woman. "I'm going to have puppies!"

•

Did you hear about the Hollywood actress who made it the hard way?

She had talent.

•

How can you be sure your girlfriend gives great head?

When you have to pull the sheets out of the crack in your ass.

•

Two real estate agents went to lunch together and were commiserating about the slow market. "If I don't sell more houses this spring," one confided over his martini, "I'm going to lose my fucking ass!"

Realizing how loudly he'd spoken, the salesman turned to a young woman at the next table with a sheepish smile. "Sorry about the bad language," he apologized.

"That's quite all right," she replied with a charming smile. "If I don't sell more fuckin' ass this spring, I'm going to lose my house."

•

What's a double-bagger?

A woman so ugly that before you'll screw her you put a bag over her head, and one over yours—just in case hers falls off.

•

Six-year-old Missy and eight-year-old Nate were having a fine time watching through the keyhole of their older sister's room as she and her boyfriend energetically went at it. She was making even more noise than usual, and finally they heard her moan, "Oh, Billy, baby, you're in me where no man has ever been before."

"Hmmmm," commented Nate, "he must be fucking her in the ass."

•

Why did the Aggie tattoo her Zip code on her inner thigh?

So she could get male in her box.

•

Why did the elderly Polish woman go to the hospital to have her tubes tied?

She decided sixteen grandchildren were enough.

•

Larry and Lucy were always hard up for cash, but were never able to stick to a savings plan. Finally Larry came up with an ingenious lay-away scheme. "I'll give you a buck every time we make love," he proposed to his wife, "and you keep it your piggy bank."

Louise agreed readily enough, and they made regular deposits for several weeks, until they couldn't resist the urge to open up the bank. And Larry was astonished when numerous fives, tens, and twenty-dollar bills also fell out on the floor. "Where'd these come from?" he asked, turning to his wife. "I only gave you a dollar each time."

"So?" said Louise. "You think everyone's as stingy as you?"

•

What do you say to a black woman who's begging you for sex?

"How much?"

•

Why do Polish babies have such big heads?

So they don't fall out during the wedding polka.

•

From within the confessional the priest was having a very hard time eliciting the comely and bashful young girl's full confession. Finally he asked her to withdraw into his chambers. "Did the young man do this to you?" asked the priest kindly, putting one arm around the girl's shoulders.

"Yes, Father," admitted the young penitent.

"I see," murmured the priest, and bent to kiss her. "And did he do this?"

"Yes, Father, and worse," said the girl, blushing a bit.

"Did he do this?" The priest lifted her skirt, pulled down her panties, and began fingering her.

"Mmmmhmmm," confirmed the girl, now turning scarlet. "And worse."

"Something like this?" quizzed the priest. Thoroughly aroused and panting heavily, he pulled the girl down onto his divan, tore off his robes, and proceeded to enter her vigorously. "Did he manage this too?"

"Yes, Father, and worse," the girl told him when he had finished.

"This too, and worse?" asked the puzzled clergyman, still breathing hard. "My dear child, what more terrible deed could the young man possibly have perpetrated?"

"You see, Father," explained the shy young penitent, "I think he's given me gonorrhea."

•

Hettie and Hiram were going at it in the cornfield one afternoon. It so happened that it had rained all night and the ground was very wet, so they found themselves sliding around in the mud quite a bit.

"Say, honey," asked Hiram after a while, "is my cock in you or in the mud?"

Hettie felt around and after a minute she answered, "Why, Hiram, it's in the mud!"

"Well, put it back in you."

After rolling around together for a few more minutes, Hiram quizzed her again. "Hettie, is it in you or in the mud?"

"In me, honey," she replied with a satisfied smile.

"Well, would you mind putting it back in the mud?"

•

Definition of a diaphragm:

A trampoline for schmucks.

•

Not long after his creation, Adam was taking a stroll around the Garden of Eden, and he noticed two birds billing and cooing up in a tree. Adam called up, "Hey, what're those two birds doing, Lord?"

"They're making love, Adam," God told him.

A little later Adam wandered into a meadow, where he saw a bull and a cow going at it hot and heavy. "Lord, what are those animals up to?" he called.

"They're making love, Adam," God told him.

Adam thought for a minute, and then asked, "It looks kind of fun. How come I don't have anyone to make love with?"

"You've got a point there," conceded God, "and we'll do something about it. When you wake up tomorrow, things will be different."

Sure enough, when Adam woke up the next morning he found Eve asleep next to him. "Hey there," he said, "come with me." And he grabbed her hand and dragged her off into the bushes.

A few minutes later Adam emerged from the shrubbery, looking depressed. "Lord," he called up, "what's a headache?"

•

"I'm exhausted," confessed the pretty young actress to her friend. "I couldn't get to sleep till after three."

"No wonder you're beat," her friend commiserated. "Two's all I usually need."

•

The farm boy got hitched, and he couldn't wait to tell his best friend about the wedding night. "Boy, is Lucille dumb," he chortled. "She put a pillow under her ass instead of her head!"

•

After servicing some thirty men in the course of a Saturday night, a Scandinavian prostitute had a heart attack and died. She went straight up to Heaven and was greeted by the great god Thor, who immediately made a pass at her. And when she rebuffed his advances, Thor proclaimed, "You cannot reject the king of the gods —I am Thor!"

"You're Thor?" snarled the hooker. "After thirty guys in a row, I'm the one who's sore."

•

Did you hear about the girl who was so fat she couldn't get out of bed?

She kept rocking herself back to sleep.

•

How is a woman like a bank?

She loses interest when you withdraw your assets.

•

Sally was talking with her rather naive young friend Susie, and the topic came around to sex. "You ought to make that big galoot of yours pay you a little something each time," advised Sally.

"Pay me? Why on earth, when I have just as much fun doing it as he does?" wondered Susie.

"That's not the point. You'll keep having fun, and you'll end up with a little spending money, honey."

So Susie thought it over, and when her boyfriend Phil came over she told him it wasn't going to be free anymore. "Gee, baby, how come?" he asked, puzzled. "I thought you liked it."

"I like it fine, but I'm not giving it away anymore," she explained.

"Well, how much do you expect me to pay?" asked Phil.

"Whatever you think's it's worth," Susie said coyly, and led him into the bedroom. They screwed furiously all through the rainy night, Phil being determined to get his money's worth and Susie pleased to be making some money. When she woke in the morning Phil had already left, and on the bedside table was a shiny new quarter.

Scooping it up and humming a happy little tune, Susie got dressed and walked to church, a big smile on her face. The ground was still wet, with sunlight reflecting on the many puddles, and as she stepped across a particularly wide one, Susie saw the reflection of her pussy. Pointing at it playfully, she said with a wink, "Why hello there, you little moneymaker."

•

What brilliant marketing idea did the madam of the whorehouse come up with?

Scratch 'n' sniff business cards.

•

Know what "coyote ugly" means?

It's a girl so ugly that when you look at her

head on your shoulder in the morning light, you gnaw the arm off rather than wake her up.

•

Maisie was by far the bustiest and best-looking girl in the whorehouse. Often she'd pick up as many as ten or twelve men a night, leading them up the two flights of stairs to her palatial room on the top floor, and on weekends she'd sometimes see as many as twenty-five a night. So the madam was completely taken by surprise when Maisie told her she was quitting. "Whatever for?" asked the older woman. "At the rate you're going, why you'll be able to retire in another year or two with a nice nest egg."

"I know," sighed Maisie, "but it's not worth it. It's wearing me out."

"Well, honey, you don't have to work quite so hard," the madam pointed out. "Why don't you cut back to ten fellers a night or so?"

"Oh, it's not the men," exclaimed Maisie. "Those stairs are killing me."

•

Chinese for pussy: Tong chow.
Chinese word for bad pussy: Tong chow yuk.

•

A hen and a duck were passing the time of day in the barnyard, and during the course of

114

the conversation the duck asked the hen what price her eggs were fetching at the market.

"Seventy-five cents a dozen," the hen told her. "How about yours?"

"Eighty-five cents," answered the duck proudly. "Of course, mine are larger."

"Huh," clucked the hen, moving off. "I wouldn't stretch my twat for a dime."

●

What do you call a stewardess who gives a passenger a hand job?

A highjacker.

●

What's a lap dog?

An ugly woman who gives good head.

●

The penny-pinching Scotsman absolutely refused to pay the whorehouse's standard fee of fifty dollars. In fact he drew the line at twenty-five dollars, but after much haggling he and the madam agreed on thirty dollars and he went upstairs with one of the girls. She was astonished when he began to fuck her bellybutton. "What the hell are you doing?" she protested. "You might be more satisfied if you move down a bit, pal."

"I know, I know," muttered the Scotsman,

"but for thirty dollars I want a hole that's all my own."

•

A Cockney fellow decided to visit the United States, and when he reached New York he was quite overcome by the number of good-looking women walking around the city. One breezy morning he decided to muster his courage and try to pick one of them up, so he followed a redhead onto the Third Avenue bus. "Kind of airy isn't it?" he asked, just as the woman reached the top of the steps.

"Sure is, buddy," returned the New Yorker without missing a beat. "What'd you expect— ostrich feathers?"

•

Did you hear about the one-legged Iranian woman who was gang-raped?

She couldn't cross her legs to save her ass.

•

How about the Iraqi who came back very disappointed from the imported-car dealership?

He thought a vulva was a fancy car from Sweden.

•

The madam hired a local carpenter to install a partition between two rooms, and when the work was done he informed her that the cost was sixty dollars.

"I don't have sixty dollars," said the madam with a coy smile, "but you're welcome to take it in trade."

The carpenter thought it over for a moment and then agreed, providing she'd do the servicing herself. "Why, sure," said the madam, rather flattered, and led him back to her boudoir and undressed. In no time flat the carpenter had his thumb up her pussy and index finger up her asshole.

"Gimme the sixty bucks now," he hissed, "or I pull out the partition."

•

Pete and Joe had grown up together and kept in touch, even though Pete had become a respected small-town doctor and Joe a flamboyant homosexual. Finally Joe decided to visit his old friend, and was intrigued by a collection of funny-looking wrinkled objects on display in the doctor's office. "What're those?" he asked.

"Petrified pussies," explained Pete proudly. "The world's definitive collection, and I don't mind telling you they represent quite an investment of time and money."

"Is that so?" Joe went slowly around the room, wetting his finger, rubbing each specimen, and touching his finger to his lips. At long last he turned to his old friend. "I'm sorry to be the bearer of bad tidings," he said gravely, "but you've been cheated. Someone's slipped in two assholes on you."

•

What's the ultimate in embarrassment for a woman?

When her Ben-Wa balls set off the metal detector at the airport.

•

Mrs. Goldfarb had an absolutely enormous vagina, and finally the unsatisfied Mr. Goldfarb decided to take his wife to a plastic surgeon. The doctor had no experience in this particular surgery, but being a creative sort, he grafted one of the woman's ears to the orifice and the operation appeared to be a complete success.

Three weeks later she arrived at his office for a follow-up visit. "And how do you feel, Mrs. Goldfarb?" inquired the doctor, beaming genially across the desk at his star patient. "Have you had any pain?"

Mrs. Goldfarb lifted her leg, hoisted her skirts, and replied, "Please, doctor, could you speak up?"

•

Mr. McInerney had been dead for over a year and his life had been made miserable by his wife's constant nagging, but neither of these facts prevented his widow from gushing on and on at the slightest opportunity about her late husband's virtues. It was the parish priest who bore the brunt of this, and finally he'd had enough. At the church picnic Mrs. McInerny soon cornered him by the lemonade and began the litany of her husband's virtues. "Such a good man, so kind, so gentle," she rhapsodized, "and you know, Father, he never laid a hand on me. Never touched a hair of me. Never a hair—"

"What marksmanship!" interrupted the priest.

•

What do Tupperware and male walruses have in common?

They both like a tight seal.

•

When Mr. Pilkington showed up at the corner barbershop for his customary shave, the barber pointed out a curly blonde hair in his mustache.

"Ah," said Mr. Pilkington, leaning back in the chair, "that's because I always give my little wife a kiss on the head before I leave for work."

"I see," said the barber. "But Mr. Pilkington, there's shit all over your necktie."

●

Smith came home early one day, only to find his new bride firmly grasping the penises of two of his friends with each hand, receiving a third man from the rear, and going down on a fourth man who lay moaning beneath her.

"Oh, darling, how could you?" asked her husband reprovingly.

"You know, dear," she answered, looking up briefly, "I've always been something of a flirt."

●

What's the difference between a pussy and a cunt?

A pussy is soft, warm, inviting . . . and a cunt is the person who owns it.

●

Why don't girls drink beer on the beach?

They might get sand in their Schlitz.

●

The playboy encountered a lovely young thing on one of his trips abroad and decided to marry her. Blessing the fact that she was not only a virgin but totally naive, he seized on the wedding night as a chance to break her in right, and had her suck him off a number of times.

The next day the bride went to see her mother, and burst into tears almost immediately. "Oh, Mother," she sobbed, "I did so want to have children, and now I just know I never shall."

"Now, now, dear, what makes you so sure?" asked the mother soothingly.

"Because," she wept, "because I'll never learn to swallow that dreadful stuff!"

•

The prostitute had her period, but she was short of cash and unwilling to turn away a customer. When the lights were out she pulled out her protective sponge and put it on the bedside table, and the farmer she was servicing did the same with his wad of chewing tobacco. After they were finished, the whore reached over and stuck the tobacco inside her, while the farmer began chewing on the sponge.

"You bastard!" she cried when the tobacco began to sting. "I think you've given me syphilis."

The farmer spat skeptically. Seeing the blood, he sat bolt upright and yelled, "Don't you complain, bitch—you've given me TB!"

•

What do you call a female sex-change operation?

An addadicktome.

•

What's the difference between eating pussy and eating sushi?

The rice.

•

The big attraction at the County Fair was a certain cow, installed in considerable secrecy in its own tent and reputed to be worth over a million dollars. Finally Jim-Bob gave into his curiosity and shelled out the five dollar admission fee, only to be confronted with a perfectly ordinary-looking cow. In answer to his question, the cow handler explained in a stage whisper, "The reason that cow's worth so much is that she has a pussy just like a woman's. Lift up her tail and see for yourself."

Jim-Bob did exactly that, after which he was overcome by such a fit of laughter that he eventually collapsed on the ground, gasping for air and clutching his sides. When he was finally able to sit up and wipe the tears from his eyes, he explained, still chuckling, "And to think my wife has a pussy just like a cow's, and it ain't worth a nickel."